The Clever Teens' Tales From World War One

Felix Rhodes

Copyright © 2020 Felix Rhodes

All rights reserved.
ISBN- 978-1-8380134-8-6

Complete Series:

The Clever Teens' Guide to World War One
The Clever Teens' Guide to World War Two
The Clever Teens' Guide to the Russian Revolution
The Clever Teens' Guide to Nazi Germany
The Clever Teens' Guide to the Cold War

The Clever Teens' Tales From World War One
The Clever Teens' Tales From World War Two
The Clever Teens' Tales From the Cold War

Contents

The Assassination of an Archduke	1
The Schlieffen Plan	8
Gavrilo Princip	11
The Execution of a British Soldier	14
The Execution of a German Spy	17
John French	22
Gallipoli	25
Gas	29
The Sinking of the Lusitania	35
The Execution of Edith Cavell	40
The Battle of Verdun	45
Horatio Kitchener	48
The Battle of the Somme	53
Douglas Haig	58
Mata Hari	64
Winston Churchill	67
Kaiser Wilhelm II	73
Georges Clemenceau	79
World War One Memorial Plaques	83
The Treaty of Versailles	85
Woodrow Wilson	90
The League of Nations	94
Spiritualism	97
The Unknown Warrior	105

The Clever Teens' Tales
From World War One

28 June 1914
The Assassination of an Archduke

On Sunday, 28 June 1914, the fifty-year-old heir to the Austrian-Hungarian throne, the Archduke Franz Ferdinand and his wife, the Countess Sophie, paid an official visit to Sarajevo, capital of Bosnia, to inspect troops of the Austrian-Hungarian army. And it was the assassination of Franz Ferdinand and his wife on this day in this city that would unleash a chain of events that rapidly escalated into the most devastating war the world had seen – the First World War.

Archduke in love

The Emperor of the Austrian-Hungarian (Habsburg) Empire, Franz Joseph, had ruled since 1848, and would do so until his death in 1916, aged eighty-six, a rule of sixty-eight years. When, in 1899, his nephew and heir presumptive, Archduke Franz Ferdinand, announced his desire to marry Sophie Chotek, a Czech, it sent shockwaves through the royal family. For Sophie, although a countess, was a commoner. But the archduke was in love and no amount of family pressure would dissuade him from taking her hand. They married on 28 June 1900. Sophie, as a non-royal, would never become queen, and the archduke had to sign away the right of his future children to succeed him. To add to the indignity, Sophie was barred from attending royal occasions, the only exception was in regard to the archduke's position of field marshal when, acting under his military capacity, he was allowed to have his wife at his side. Thus, together, on 28 June 1914, they made their way to Sarajevo.

The Black Hand

Six years previously, Bosnia had been annexed to the Habsburg Empire. Aggrieved Bosnian Serbs dreamt of freedom and incorporation into the nation of Serbia. The 28 June was also a significant day for Serbia – it was their national holiday and the anniversary of the 1389 Battle of Kosovo, in which Serbia was defeated by the Turks. Thus, the chosen date was provocative, and the Austrians knew it. The Serbs warned the Austrians against the visit, saying that the archduke would be putting himself in danger. One Serb freedom fighter / terrorist, Borivoje Jevtic, wrote 'How dared Franz Ferdinand, not only the representative of the oppressor but in his own person an arrogant tyrant, enter Sarajevo on that day?' Only in 1878, after five hundred years of Turkish rule, had Serbia gained its independence – but not the Bosnian Serbs who remained first under Turkish rule, then, from 1908, Austrian-Hungarian rule.

A Serbian nationalistic group calling itself the Black Hand decided to strike at the hated Austrian-Hungarians by assassinating the heir to the Habsburg throne. (Jevtic, quoted above, was a member). Indeed, they had tried to assassinate Emperor Franz Joseph three years earlier. Dispatched to Sarajevo were a number of young freedom fighters, including a nineteen-year-old named Gavrilo Princip. And it was in Sarajevo that Princip would change the world.

Each armed with a revolver, a hand grenade and, in the event of failure, a vial of cyanide, the would-be assassins joined, at various intervals, the mass of spectators lined along a six-kilometre route and waited for the six-car motorcade to come into view. The first lost his nerve, whilst the second, Nedeljko Čabrinović, managed to throw his bomb causing injury to a driver and a few spectators but leaving the archduke and his wife unharmed. Čabrinović swallowed his cyanide and jumped into the River Miljacka behind. But the poison, so old, failed to work and the river only came up to his ankles. Arrested, he was attacked by several bystanders. Meanwhile, Princip, witnessing the failure of the mission, traipsed to a local inn.

Understandably shaken, Franz Ferdinand arrived, as planned, at the City Hall, where he complained to the city mayor, 'Mr Mayor, I come to Sarajevo on a visit, and I get bombs thrown at me. It is outrageous.' Then, in delivering a speech, he ended with the words, 'I see in the people of Sarajevo an expression of joy at the failure of the attempt at assassination'.

Franz Ferdinand, Library of Congress.

On the countess's suggestion, Franz Ferdinand decided to visit the injured lying in hospital. On the way, his chauffeur took a wrong turning and found himself the wrong way down a one-way street, ironically named after the emperor, Franz Josef. On realizing his error, the chauffeur tried to reverse the car but stalled next to the very inn where Princip was planning his next move.

On seeing the archduke's car in front of him, Princip jumped onto its running board and fired, hitting the countess in the stomach. 'Sophie, don't die,' wailed the archduke, 'stay alive for the children'. The second bullet caught him in the throat.

One of the royal couple's bodyguards, Count Franz von Harrach, riding on the car's running board, gave this account: 'As the car quickly reversed, a thin stream of blood spurted from His Highness's mouth onto my right check. As I was pulling out my handkerchief to wipe the blood away from his mouth, the Duchess cried out to him, "In Heaven's name, what has happened to you?" At that she slid off the seat and lay on the floor of the car, with her face between his knees. I had no idea that she too was hit and thought she had simply fainted with fright.'

The arrest of Gavrilo Princip, 28 June 1914.

As the car hurried to the governor's residence, a member of his staff asked the archduke if he was OK, to which the archduke replied several times, 'It is nothing', before breathing his last.

Princip was bundled to the ground, his revolver seized from his hand. He managed to swallow the cyanide but, again, the poison, being so old, had no affect. (Although happy to have assassinated Franz Ferdinand, Princip was sorry to have killed the archduke's wife).

The Road to War

Austria reeled in shock, the assassination prompting several anti-Serb demonstrations. Serbia's government denied any involvement. Since 1912, Austria-Hungary had been concerned with Serbia's growing military strength so the crime presented the perfect opportunity for the Habsburg Empire to affirm its authority over its neighbour. With the backing of its powerful ally, Germany, Austria-Hungary sent a ten-point ultimatum to Serbia which, in the words of Britain's foreign secretary, Sir Edward Grey, was the 'most formidable document ever sent from one nation to another'. Serbia had 48 hours to respond. Shocked by the demands of the 'July Ultimatum', as it became known, Serbia turned to its ally, Russia, who recommended complete acceptance. Unable to do so entirely, Serbia agreed to eight, suggesting, quite reasonably, that the Hague Tribunal decide the other two. Not good enough, said the Austrian-Hungarians, breaking off diplomatic relations. On 28 July they declared war on Serbia.

And now, all the alliances formed in the preceding decades fell into place. Russia, protector of Serbia, began to mobilise. France, Russia's ally in the Triple Entente, felt obliged to offer its support. Germany gave Russia twelve hours to halt its mobilisation. The deadline passed, thus on 1 August, Germany declared war on Russia and, two days later, on France. 'The sword has been forced into our hand,' claimed the Kaiser.

Germany's determination to invade France through Belgium brought in Great Britain, who in 1839 had signed a treaty guaranteeing Belgium neutrality. Would Britain really risk war with a 'kindred nation' over a 'scrap of paper', a treaty signed seventy-five years before? Britain prevaricated but yes, it would, declaring war on Germany on 4 August.

For the Russian, British and German sovereigns, the prospect of war was akin to a family spat – Wilhelm II, of the Hohenzollern dynasty, was Queen Victoria's grandson and a cousin either by marriage or blood to both the Russian Tsar, Nicholas II, and Britain's King George V.

Within a matter of weeks, what started off as 'some damn foolish thing in the Balkans', as the former German chancellor, Otto von Bismarck, had once predicted, had escalated into a major conflict, one that would last 1,568 days, from 28 July 1914 to 11 November 1918, and cost over nine million lives. The Great War had begun.

July 1914
The Schlieffen Plan

Germany now faced a war on both its western and eastern borders; a war on two fronts. But it was a prospect they had long anticipated. In 1905, the then German Chief of Staff, Count Alfred von Schlieffen, had devised a plan for such an eventuality. Russia, he surmised, not incorrectly, would take up to six weeks to mobilise its armies, allowing Germany time to defeat France. In order to avoid the line of fortifications on the Franco–German border, the German army would have to advance through neutral Belgium in a huge sweeping movement: 'let the last man on the right brush the Channel with his sleeve'. Having knocked out Belgium, it would swing south, covering twenty kilometres a day, and encircle Paris. Having dealt with the French, it would then have time to move east to confront the vast armies of Russia. Schlieffen died in 1913. One year later, his grand plan was put into action.

Count Alfred von Schlieffen

'Poor little Belgium'

Speed was of the essence. On 2 August, Germany stormed through Luxembourg and demanded immediate access through Belgium. But 'Poor little Belgium', as the British press called her, refused and turned to a 1839 treaty, guaranteeing its neutrality. One of the signatories was Germany. The other was Great Britain. Britain asked Germany for an assurance that they would respect Belgium's neutrality. Germany ignored it and on 4 August began bombing the Belgium city of Liège. Germany could not believe that Britain would go to war with a 'kindred nation' over a 'scrap of paper' – a treaty signed seventy-five years before. But it did – Britain declared war on

Germany on 4 August.

Sir Edward Grey, gazing out from the Foreign Office, remarked, 'the lamps are going out all over Europe. We shall not see them lit again in our lifetime'.

'It'll all be over by Christmas'

Grey, in his gloominess, was in a minority – the rest of Europe rejoiced at the prospect of war. Everywhere, civilians gathered in town squares to celebrate, young men anticipated adventures of daring-do and chivalry. 'It'll all be over by Christmas', the British army was told; 'you'll be home before the leaves fall', declared the Kaiser to his troops. For Russia, a victorious war would stifle the murmurings of revolution that was infecting the tsar's kingdom. For France, still chafing over its defeat in the Franco–Prussian War in 1871, war offered a chance to re-establish its reputation.

The Great War had begun.

Gavrilo Princip

In the annals of notoriety, the name Gavrilo Princip should perhaps rank higher than it does. For this nineteen-year-old Serb committed a crime that, without overestimating the fact, set the agenda for the whole of the twentieth century. Princip was the man who shot and killed the heir to the Austrian-Hungarian throne, the Archduke Franz Ferdinand.

Exactly one month after the assassination, Europe was at war, a war that quickly spread and became the Great War, or, as we know it, the First World War. And from the post-war seeds of discontent came the rise of Nazism and the road to the Second World War.

Born to an impoverished family in Bosnia on 25 July 1894, Gavrilo Princip was one of nine children, six of whom died during infancy. Suffering from tuberculosis, the frail and slight Princip learnt to read, the first in his family to do so, and devoured the histories of the Serbs and their oppression at the hands of the Ottoman and Habsburg Empires.

The Black Hand

In 1911, a friend of Gavrilo Princip's, Bogdan Zerajic, had tried to assassinate the Austrian-Hungarian governor of Bosnia. He failed and ended up shooting himself. But it provided the young Princip with an inspiration. He tried to enlist in various terrorist groups but was turned down due to his short stature

Eventually he was accepted and tasked to join a group called the Black Hand. Its explicit purpose was the assassination of Archduke Franz Ferdinand. The opportunity – the occasion of the archduke's visit to the Bosnian capital of Sarajevo, due for 28 June 1914.

The plan was known to the Serbian prime minister. Although sympathetic, he feared the consequences and ordered the arrest of the Black Hand conspirators. Fatefully, his orders came too late.

The Wrong Turn

Having assassinated the archduke and his wife, Gavrilo Princip tried to shoot himself but was wrestled to the ground where again he tried to kill himself by swallowing his cyanide pill. But the poison, so old, failed to work.

At the time of the assassination, Gavrilo Princip was a month short of his twentieth birthday. His age saved him from execution as Austrian-Hungarian law decreed that the death penalty could not be applied to those aged under 20. After a 12-day trial, Princip was sentenced instead to the maximum penalty of twenty years to be served at Theresienstadt prison (later used by the Nazis as a death camp). While in prison, he suffered a resurgence of his tuberculosis and, due to the poor hygiene and the inadequate diet, had to have an arm amputated. His condition worsened and he died in the prison hospital, aged twenty-three, on 28 April 1918.

After the war, his remains were re-interred in St Mark's Cemetery in Sarajevo.

Gavrilo Princip's gun; the car in which the Archduke and the countess was riding; and his bloodstained sky blue uniform and plumed cocked hat are all on permanent display in the Museum of Military History in Vienna, Austria.

8 September 1914
The Execution of a British Soldier

On 5 September 1914, the first day of the Battle of Marne, Thomas Highgate, a nineteen-year-old British private, was found hiding in a barn dressed in civilian clothes. Highgate was tried by court martial, convicted of desertion and, in the early hours of 8 September, was executed by firing squad. His was the first of 306 executions carried out by the British during the First World War.

Thomas Highgate was born in Shoreham in Kent on 13 May 1895. In February 1913, aged seventeen, he joined the Royal West Kent Regiment. Within months, Highgate fell foul of the military authorities – in 1913, he was upbraided for being late for tattoo (a military display of music and marching), and 'exchanging duties without permission'. In early 1914, he was reprimanded for having a rusty rifle and deserting for which he received the punishment of forty-eight days detention.

First Battle of the Marne

On 5 September, the first day of the Battle of the Marne and the 35th day of the war, Private Highgate's nerves got the better of him and he fled the battlefield. He hid in a barn in the village of Tournan, a few miles south of the river, and was discovered wearing civilian clothes by a gamekeeper who happened to be English and an ex-soldier. Quite where Highgate obtained his civilian clothes is not recorded but the gamekeeper spotted his uniform lying in a heap nearby. Highgate confessed, 'I have had enough of it, I want to get out of it and this is how I am going to do it'.

Having been turned in, Highgate was tried by a court martial for desertion. The trial, presided over by three officers, was brief. Highgate did not speak and was not represented. He was found guilty. At 6.20 on the morning of 8 September, Highgate was informed that he would be executed. The execution was carried out fifty minutes later – at 7.07, he was shot by firing squad.

Highgate's name is shown on the British memorial to the missing at La Ferté-sous-Jouarre on the south bank of the River Marne. The memorial features the names of over 3,000 British soldiers with no known grave.

Shoreham

By the time the war had ended, Highgate's parents had moved away from Shoreham, settling in Crayford in southeast London. Highgate had four brothers, two of whom were also killed during the war. Their names, including that of Thomas, appear on the Sidcup war memorial.

In 2000, the parish council in Highgate's home village of Shoreham replaced its war memorial plaque bearing the names of those who had fallen during the war of 1914-1918 as the original had become worn. The original did not include Highgate's name simply because, as mentioned, the family had moved away. Nonetheless, in 2000, after some debate, the council voted not to include Highgate's name on the replacement plaque. However, a space was left should, at some point in the future, the people of Shoreham want his name added.

In November 2006, the UK government pardoned all 306 servicemen executed in the First World War but, to this day, the name Thomas Highgate still does not feature on Shoreham's war memorial.

6 November 1914
The Execution of a German Spy

Karl Lody was a German spy and the first to be executed in Britain during the First World War.

Born in Berlin on 20 January 1877, Karl Hans Lody spoke perfect English with an American accent, having been married to an American and lived in Nebraska. Having obtained a US passport under the name Charles A. Inglis, which allowed him to travel freely, Lody arrived in Edinburgh on 27 August 1914. Staying in a hotel, he hired a bicycle and cycled each day to the docks at the Firth of Forth and Rosyth's naval base, both of strategic importance during the First World War, in order to observe and take notes.

Snow on their boots

MI5, who had been monitoring letters sent abroad, intercepted Lody's very first message back to the Germans. The address in Stockholm that Lody had used was well known to MI5, instantly arousing their suspicions. But they did not arrest him immediately, preferring, instead, to monitor his activities. Lody's letters were usually signed

'Nazi', an abbreviation of the name Ignatz, the German form of Ignatius, and nothing to do with Adolf Hitler's Nazi party which did not come into existence until after the war. ('Nazi' was also a generic term for an Austro-Hungarian soldier, akin to 'Tommy' for a British soldier or 'Fritz' for a German one.)

Many of Lody's letters, some of which were coded, contained misleading information, which MI5 were more than happy to allow through. One example was Lody's assertion that thousands of Russian troops had landed in Scotland on their way to the Western Front, which may have led to the infamous 'snow on their boots' rumour that gained popular currency in wartime Britain: supposed sightings of Russian soldiers marching through Britain, so fresh from Russia that they still had the snow on their boots.

DORA

On 29 September, fearing his cover was about to be blown, Lody moved to Dublin. He travelled via Liverpool and while there made notes describing the Liverpool docks and the ships he saw. This letter, sent without coding, revealed pertinent information. It was at this point MI5 decided Lody had to be stopped.

He was arrested on 2 October in Killarney, County Kerry, from where he'd been planning on visiting Queenstown, a major naval base. Lody was charged with two offences under 'DORA', the Defence of the Realm Act, which had only come into effect two months previously – 8 August. Initially, Lody tried to pass himself off as an American citizen but police found a trove of incriminating evidence in his hotel bedroom, including drafts of his letters and telegrams.

A really fine man

Tried in public at London's Old Bailey, the case, unlike later spying trials, was widely reported in the national press. Lody was held responsible for the sinking of a British cruiser whose movements were known to Berlin thanks to his information. Lody tried to argue that he was an unwilling spy but evidence showed that he had voluntarily signed an agreement with the German admiralty. He refused to name his contact in Berlin: 'That name I cannot say as I have given my word of honour'. His activities, he said, would 'hopefully save my country, but probably not me'. Lody's gentlemanly conduct in court won him much admiration in Britain. But it came as no surprise when on 2 November Karl Lody was found guilty and sentenced to death.

Sir Vernon Kell, head of MI5, described Lody as a 'really fine man', and he 'felt it deeply that so brave a man should have to pay the death penalty.'

The death sentence was approved by King George V.

On the day before his execution, Lody wrote a number of letters. One, to the commanding officer at the Tower of London, thanks him and his staff for their 'kind and considered treatment.' In another, to his family in Stuttgart, Lody writes, 'My hour has come, and I must start on the journey through the Dark Valley like so many of my comrades in this terrible War of Nations.'

A brave man

Karl Lody was executed on the morning of 6 November 1914. When the warder came to take him from his cell, Lody asked him, 'I suppose you will not care to shake hands with a German spy?' To which, the officer replied, 'No. But I will shake hands with a brave man.'

'To the very end,' wrote the *Daily Mail*, 'Lody maintained the calm imperturbability which characterized him throughout the three day's trial.' A warder, describing Lody's walk to face execution, wrote that the condemned man seemed 'unconcerned as though he was going to a tea party'. Refusing to be blindfolded, Lody sat down on the wooden chair, folded his arms and crossed his legs. He was executed by an eight-man firing squad.

Karl Lody was the first of eleven German spies to be

executed in Britain during the war, and the first person to be executed at the Tower of London since 1747, one hundred and sixty-seven years before.

John French

During the war, Britain had two commander-in-chiefs; the first, Sir John French, held the position from the start of the war until December 1915 and then Douglas Haig who held the position until the end of the war.

John French spent much of his early military career, like many of his contemporaries, in Africa and India. He was part of the failed 1884/5 mission to relieve General Gordon in the Sudan; and from 1891 served in India.

In India, French first met his future rival, Douglas Haig, then a captain. Indeed, Haig later lent French a large sum of money to help the latter stave off bankruptcy. While in India, French had an affair with the wife of a fellow officer. The scandal almost ended his career. He survived and went on to serve with distinction as a cavalry officer during the Boer War where, most notably, in 1900, under the stewardship of Frederick Roberts, he lead the force that relieved the British garrison besieged in the town of Kimberley.

French was appointed Britain's army chief-of-staff in 1911 and given command of the British Expeditionary Force, the BEF. In 1913, he was promoted to the rank of field marshal.

1914

With the outbreak of war in 1914, the BEF crossed the Channel, landing on the continent on 7 August. (Consisting of little more than 90,000 men, only half of whom were regular soldiers; the other half being reservists, the BEF had famously, and allegedly, been dismissed by the Kaiser, Wilhelm II, who, on 19 August, ordered his army to 'exterminate the treacherous English and walk over General French's contemptible little army.' Hence British soldiers took pride in calling themselves the 'Old Contemptibles'.) French's orders, from Horatio Kitchener, minister for war, were to work alongside the French but not to take orders from them. The BEF first saw action during the Battle of Mons, 23 August 1914, Britain's first battle in Western Europe since Waterloo ninety-nine years before.

Following the Allies' Retreat from Mons and with the Germans advancing on Paris, Joseph Joffre, the French commander-in-chief, decided to counterattack, aided by the British. But French, concerned for his exhausted men, even at the cost of French soldiers, instead contemplated a complete withdrawal. On 1 September French received a visit in person from Kitchener who ordered him to obey Joffre's commands.

1915

1915, a year of continuous stalemate, and the disastrous Battle of Loos, did little for the failing reputation of French, whose mood swung from one extreme to another. In December 1915, he was told to resign and was replaced as commander-in-chief by his deputy, Sir Douglas Haig.

By way of compensation, French was showered with various titles and awards, and given command of the British Home Forces until 1918, during which time he had to deal with the 1916 Easter Rising in Ireland.

French, resentful that he had been usurped by his former deputy, devoted much energy to criticizing Haig, to the point he was summoned to Buckingham Palace and told, in person by the king, to desist.

John French died on 22 May 1925, aged seventy-two.

French's older sister, Charlotte Despard, was a constant embarrassment to him. She was, at various times, a suffragette, a Labour Party candidate, a pacifist, an Irish republican, a member of *Sinn Féin*, a vegetarian, a fan of Mahatma Gandhi, a communist and an admirer of the Soviet Union. One thing that remained constant in her life was Despard's animosity towards her famous brother.

17 February 1915
The Start of the Gallipoli Campaign

In November 1914, the Ottoman Empire, entered the war on the side of the Central Powers and on Christmas Day went on the offensive against the Russians, launching an attack through the Caucasus. Russia's Tsar Nicholas II sent an appeal to Britain, asking for a diversionary attack that would ease the pressure on Russia. From this came the ill-fated Gallipoli Campaign.

Naval Assault

The British planned its diversionary attack, to use the Royal Navy to take control of the Dardanelles Straits from where they could attack Constantinople, the Ottoman capital. By capturing Constantinople, the British hoped then to link up with their Russian allies. The attack would, it hoped, have the additional benefit of drawing German troops away from both the Western and Eastern Fronts.

The Dardanelles, a strait of water separating mainland Turkey and the Gallipoli peninsula, is sixty miles long and, at its widest, only 3.5 miles. Britain's First Lord of the Admiralty, Winston Churchill, insisted that the Royal Navy, acting alone, could succeed. On 19 February, a flotilla of British and French ships pounded the outer forts of the Dardanelles and a month later attempted to penetrate the strait. It failed, losing six ships (three sunk and three damaged), two thirds of its fleet. Soldiers, it was decided, would be needed after all.

ANZACs

Lord Kitchener put in charge Sir Ian Hamilton, but sent him into battle with out of date maps, inaccurate information and inexperienced troops. A force of British, French and ANZAC (Australian and New Zealand Army Corp) troops landed on the Gallipoli peninsula on 25 April 1915. The Turks, who, led by Mustafa Kemal Atatürk, had had time to prepare, were waiting for them in the hills above the beaches and unleashed a volley of fire that kept the Allied troops pinned down on the sand. The ANZACs managed to gain a foothold on what became known as 'Anzac Cove' but under sustained fire and faced with steep cliffs, were unable to push inland. The British, likewise, were unable to make any headway.

As on the Western Front, stalemate ensued. The Turks were not the pushover the British had hoped for. The Allies, under constant attack, took cover as best as they could among the rocks, with only the beach behind them and, without shade, exposed to searing sun. Their fallen comrades lay putrefied and bloated beside them, the stench filling the air.

Sulva Bay

On 6 August, the British launched a renewed attack. The ANZACs would attempt to break out from their beach and take the high ground whilst a British contingent of 20,000 new troops led by General Sir Frederick Stopford would land on Sulva Bay on the north side of Gallipoli.

Stopford's men made a successful landing, outnumbering the enemy by fifteen to one. But instead of pressing home their advantage, the general gave his men the afternoon off to enjoy the sun while he had a snooze. Hamilton advised but did not order an advance. By the time Stopford did advance, it was too late – the Turks had rushed men into position and the stalemate of before prevailed.

The Allied troops endured further months of misery. Seventy percent of the ANZACs suffered from dysentery, where medical care, unlike the Western Front, was at best primitive.

Evacuation

With the onset of winter, the troops, without shelter and exposed to the elements, suffered frostbite. In October, Hamilton was replaced by Charles Monro, who recommended an end to the campaign. Kitchener was dispatched by the British government to check on the situation. Appalled at what he saw and persuaded by Monro, he returned to London and urged evacuation. Finally, in January 1916, the curtain fell on the whole sorry 'side show', the last troops leaving on 9 January.

The campaign had indeed diverted Turkish forces away from Russia but it was considered a complete failure, one that cost 140,000 Allied casualties. Churchill, contrite, resigned and punished himself by joining a company of Royal Scot Fusiliers on the Western Front. (He returned to politics a year later and in 1917 was appointed Minister of Munitions). Meanwhile, Kitchener, who had been progressively side-lined, was sent on a diplomatic mission to Russia. On 5 June 1916, his ship, the HMS *Hampshire*, hit a German mine off the Orkney Islands and sunk. His body was never found.

The failure of Gallipoli also heralded the end of Herbert Asquith as prime minister – on 25 May 1915, his Liberal government was forced into a coalition, and on 5 December 1916, he was replaced as prime minister by David Lloyd George.

25 April, the date the ANZACs initially landed in Gallipoli in 1915, is now marked annually as a day of remembrance, known as Anzac Day.

22 April 1915
Fritz Haber and the First Successful Gas Attack

On 22 April 1915, during the Second Battle of Ypres, French and Algerian soldiers, fighting together, noticed a strange yellow-grey-coloured cloud floating across no man's land in their direction. As it descended over them, many collapsed, coughing and wheezing, gasping for air, frothing at the mouth. Men nearby watched as their colleagues fell to the ground in agony yet there were no gunshots to be heard and they appeared not to be visibly wounded in any way. Seized by panic, they bolted, throwing away their rifles, and even their tunics so that they might run faster, leaving a hole some four miles wide. But the Germans, wary of stepping into the cloud of poison gas protected only by their crude gasmasks, felt unable to exploit the opportunity. This, with 400 tones of chlorine gas, was the world's first successful chemical weapon attack, resulting in 6,000 casualties, mostly from asphyxia.

This new terrible weapon was inhumane, cried the Allied generals, only to be using it themselves within five months. Britain's first use of chlorine gas, at the Battle of Loos in September 1915, was not a great success. Sir John French and the British commanders had banned the use of the word 'gas', believing it too provocative a word; instead they called it the 'accessory', a vague euphemism if ever there was one. Having waited for a favourable wind, they released the gas from cylinders. But the wind turned and the gas ended up causing greater causalities among the British than it did the Germans.

*Detail from John Singer Sargent's 'Gassed', 1919.
Google Arts Project.*

Arthur Empey, an American fighting with the British, described a gas attack: 'German gas is heavier than air and soon fills the trenches and dugouts, where it has been known to lurk for two or three days, until the air is purified by means of large chemical sprayers. A company man on our right was too slow in getting on his helmet; he sank to the ground, clutching at his throat, and after a few spasmodic twistings, went West (died). It was horrible to see him die, but we were powerless to help him. In the corner of a traverse, a little, muddy cur dog, one of the company's pets, was lying dead, with his two paws over his nose. It's the animals that suffer the most, the horses, mules, cattle, dogs, cats, and rats, they having no helmets to save them.'

Fritz Haber

Fritz Haber, 1919. The Nobel Foundation.

The pioneer of poison gas was a German called Fritz Haber, a Jew who, conscious of the anti-Semitism already prevalent in *fin-de-siècle* Germany, had, in 1893, converted to Christianity. Haber had developed the means to convert nitrogen in a way that it could be used to produce cheap and effective fertilizer, which greatly improved and revolutionized agricultural efficiency. As one historian put it, 'It has been claimed that as many as two out of five humans on the planet today owe their existence to the discoveries made by [this] one brilliant German chemist.' His work won Haber the Nobel Prize for Chemistry in 1918.

The use of poisonous gas in war was prohibited by the 1899 Hague Convention yet as soon as the First World War broke out Fritz Haber and his team worked on developing gas as a weapon. Haber, as a Jew, was determined to prove his devotion and loyalty to Germany. 'During peace time,' Haber once said, 'a scientist belongs to the World, but during war time he belongs to his country'. Killing enemy troops with gas was, according to Haber, no worse than blowing their heads off with artillery. For his work, Haber was personally made an honorary captain by Kaiser Wilhelm II.

Clara Immerwahr

The successful use of chlorine gas at Ypres in April 1915 was, for the Germans, and Haber in particular, an occasion for celebration. But not so for Haber's wife, Clara. Clara Immerwahr, who herself had been a successful chemist, had been appalled by her husband's work, which she saw as a perversion of science. On 2 May, at their Berlin home, Haber hosted a party. While he and his friends toasted his success, Clara took her husband's service revolver, went into their garden and shot herself in the heart. She died the following morning in the arms of her thirteen-year-old son, Hermann.

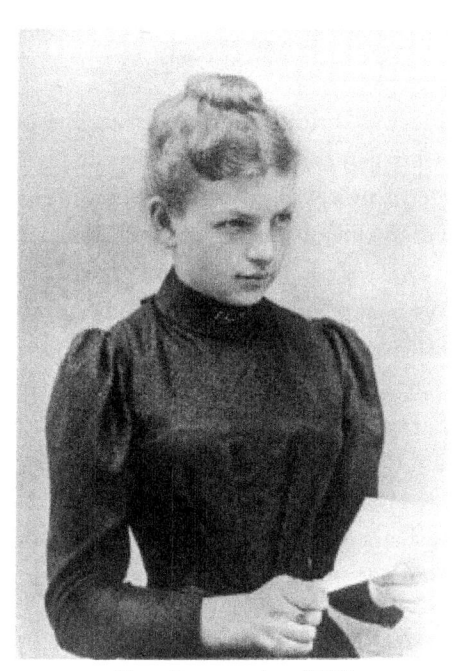

Clara Immerwahr, c1890.

Despite the setback of his wife's suicide, Haber was buoyed by his success with chlorine at Ypres but conscious of its limitations. He developed a new, more effective gas, called phosgene, which omitted a smell akin to hay. Its first use, on the Eastern front, in January 1916, proved successful. Those inflicted often showed no immediate ill effects but then would succumb, violently, some 48 hours later.

In 1917, the Germans introduced mustard gas, so named because of its odour, which could penetrate clothing and be absorbed through skin. Gas had become a common feature by the end of the war and although it was effective at incapacitating troops and causing long-term illness, gas accounted for only three percent of fatalities.

Post-war

Following the war, Fritz Haber continued his work. But, despite his Christian conversion, and despite his efforts on behalf of Germany's war efforts, he was still a Jew, and hence felt very vulnerable once, in 1933, Hitler had come to power. On seeing many of his Jewish colleagues harassed, mistreated and dismissed, Haber resigned. He emigrated to England in 1933 but, after only four months, decided to start afresh in Palestine. Stopping off in Basel in Switzerland, Haber, aged sixty-five, died of a heart attack on 29 January 1934.

His son, Hermann, later emigrated to the US where, apparently ashamed by his father's work, he committed suicide in 1946.

Zyklon B

But the most tragic irony was that in his agricultural research, Haber helped develop pesticide gases, which included a cyanide-based pesticide called Zyklon B; indeed one of his assistants was credited as the official inventor of Zyklon B. Zyklon B was the main component used by the Nazis in their death camps. Among the six million killed in the gas chambers during the Holocaust were several members of Fritz Haber's extended family, including several of his nieces and nephews.

7 May 1915
The Sinking of the Lusitania

On the 7 May 1915, a German U-boat sunk the British luxury liner, the RMS *Lusitania*. 1,198 people lost their lives, including 128 Americans. Its sinking caused moral outrage both in Britain and in the US and led, ultimately, to the USA declaring war against Germany.

The 'Great War' was still less than a year old. On 18 February 1915, in response to Great Britain's blockade of Germany, the Germans announced that it would, in future, be operating a policy of 'unrestricted submarine warfare'. In other words, German U-boats would actively seek out and attack enemy shipping within the war zone of British waters. Even ships displaying a neutral flag, they announced, would be at risk – the Germans being aware of the British habit of sailing under a neutral flag.

The *Lusitania* was certainly not the first victim of Germany's new policy – on 28 March 1915, the British ship RMS *Falaba* was torpedoed and sunk by German U-boat off the coast of southern Ireland. 104 people were killed, including one American.

Liable to destruction

Wealthy passengers boarding the Lusitania, a 32,000-ton luxury Cunard liner, in New York saw an advertisement issued by the US German embassy warning them of the risk:

Vessels flying the flag of Great Britain, or any of her allies, are liable to destruction in those waters and that travellers sailing in the war zone on ships of Great Britain or her allies do so at their own risk.

Yet any concern passengers may have harboured were brushed aside in the belief that the Germans would surely not target a civilian cruise liner. And also, with a top speed of twenty-one knots-per-hour, far higher than any other ship at the time, the *Lusitania* could easily outpace a German U-boat with a top speed of a paltry thirteen knots.

Carrying 1,959 people (1,257 passengers and 702 crew), the *Lusitania* left New York on its 202nd Atlantic crossing on 1 May 1915. The British, knowing of the potential danger as the ship approached the Ireland, gave the captain, William Thomas Turner, specific instructions. He was told that as he approached the coast he should sail at top speed and in a zigzag fashion, hence making it far more difficult for a U-boat to score a direct hit. But with thick fog and poor visibility, and wanting to save fuel, Captain Turner sailed at only fifteen knots per hour and, fatefully, in a straight line. He was also told to avoid Ireland's jutting coastline. Yet here he was, on the 7 May, within eleven miles off the coast of southern Ireland, within sight of the Old Head of Kinsale Lighthouse.

U-Boat

Lurking beneath the waters was the *U20*, captained by Walter Schwieger. The *U20* had already downed a few smaller vessels and now, in the early afternoon of 7 May, it spotted the *Lusitania* at a distance of about 700 metres. At 14:09, the *U20* fired a torpedo, hitting the *Lusitania* on the starboard side. Panic ensued. Seconds later a second explosion from deep down was heard. This, the second explosion, was what doomed the ship to its fate. It was assumed to be a second torpedo but this was not the case. Captain Schwieger always maintained that he had only fired the one, claiming: *"It would have been impossible for me, anyhow, to fire a second torpedo into this crowd of people struggling to save their lives"*.

The ship listed so severely to the side that the lifeboats on the port side were unreachable. Those that were dropped from the starboard side fell into the water at such a distance from the ship that people were forced into making a terrifyingly long leap in order to reach them.

The ship sunk quickly – in just eighteen minutes. It sank in a mere 90 metres of water. At the point the bow hit the sea bottom, the stern was still sticking out of the water.

Rescue ships were dispatched from the Irish port of Queenstown and arrived on the scene within two hours, and, unhindered by further attacks, managed to pick up 761 survivors. But 1,198 lives were lost, including 128 of the 197 Americans on board. 59 children and 35 babies were among the dead.

A legitimate target?

So what had caused the second explosion? Records showed that down in its hold, among all the cargo and baggage, the *Lusitania* had been carrying ammunition for over 4,000 small arms – some four million American-made bullets. It was the unforeseen detonation of all this live ammunition that caused the greatest damage. The Germans certainly maintained this was the case but the British and the Americans denied it. History has revealed that the Germans had been right, and therefore, by carrying ammunition, the ship was, under the laws of war, a legitimate target.

Nonetheless, with the US president, Woodrow Wilson, outraged by what he saw as an atrocity, the German high command rescinded its policy of unrestricted submarine warfare, although they were later to re-introduce it, on 1 February 1917. The British government condemned the 'barbarian' Germans as indeed they would five months later following the German execution of British nurse, Edith Cavell.

Historians have debated whether the *Lusitania* had been purposefully allowed to fall into a German trap and sunk as a means of persuading the US into joining the war. Up to this point, the US had firmly remained isolationist. In the event, it would be another two years, 6 April 1917, before the US joined the Allies but the sinking of the *Lusitania* and the killing of American citizens certainly played a large part in swaying the opinion of both the president and US public opinion.

Captain Turner

Captain Turner remained on the bridge of the ship until it was submerged. He then clung onto a chair in the swirling Irish waters for two hours before being rescued. He died 23 June 1933, aged seventy-seven.

12 October 1915
The Execution of British Nurse, Edith Cavell

When the First World War broke out, Edith Cavell was working as a matron in a Brussels nursing school, a school she had co-founded in 1907 and where she'd helped pioneer the importance of follow-up care. But at the time, July 1914, she was on leave, holidaying with her family in Norfolk, England. On hearing the news of war, her parents begged her not to return to Belgium – but of course she did.

Following the German occupation of Brussels, Cavell refused the German offer of a safe conduct into neutral Netherlands. She continued her work and in the process hid refugee British, Belgian and French soldiers and provided over two hundred of them the means to escape into the Netherlands from where most managed the journey back to England. Her network knew it was dangerous work and discussed whether they should continue. Cavell insisted they should: 'If we are arrested we shall be punished in any case, whether we have done much or little'. And so they carried on. With the

Germans watching the work at the hospital and its comings and goings, her arrest was inevitable. It duly came on 3 August 1915. Edith Cavell, arrested by the Germans, readily admitted her guilt.

Edith Cavell.

Patriotism is not enough

Cavell was remanded in isolation for ten weeks, not even being allowed to meet the lawyer appointed to defend her until the morning of her trial, a trial which lasted only two days. Cavell, along with 34 others also arrested, was found guilty. Her case became a *cause célèbre* but the British government, realising the Germans were acting within their own legality, was unable to intervene. However, the Americans, as neutrals, pointed to Cavell's nursing credentials and her saving of the lives of German soldiers, as well as British, but to no avail. Along with her Belgian accomplice, Philippe Baucq, the nurse was found guilty and sentenced to be shot.

*The Edith Cavell Memorial, London.
Photographed by the author.*

On the evening before her execution, Cavell was visited by an army chaplain. She told him, 'Patriotism is not enough. I must have no hatred or bitterness towards anyone.' The words are inscribed on Cavell's statue, near Trafalgar Square in London.

On 12 October 1915, about to face the firing squad, Cavell said, 'My soul, as I believe, is safe, and I am glad to die for my country'. She was forty-nine.

Judged justly

The German foreign secretary, Alfred Zimmermann, expressed pity for Cavell but added that she had been 'judged justly'. 'I can assure you,' wrote Zimmermann in a newspaper article, 'that the case was conducted with the utmost thoroughness. No war court in the world could have given any other verdict.' The fact that Cavell was a woman was of no relevance. But the decision to execute Cavell, however legal, was a localized one, unknown to the German army's High Command or Wilhelm II, the German Kaiser. On hearing of the execution the Kaiser was appalled, considering the sentence a political error.

Indeed, the British made propaganda capital out of the nurse's execution, stoking up anti-German feeling by exploiting the image of the gentle nurse slaughtered by the German barbarian. Following the backlash, all of the others had their death sentences commuted to imprisonment. In the weeks following Cavell's execution, recruitment into the British Army doubled. The name Edith became popular – Edith Piaf, born two months after Cavell's execution, was reputably named after her.

After the war, Cavell's body was brought back to England where, in May 1919, she was afforded a state funeral at Westminster Abbey in London, attended by packed streets of mourners. A statue was erected near Trafalgar Square, another in the grounds of Norwich cathedral, and a third in Paris. In June 1940, following Nazi Germany's invasion and occupation of France, Adolf Hitler personally ordered the destruction of Edith Cavell's monument. The London memorial, designed by Sir George Frampton, was not well received on its unveiling in 1920. One reviewer wrote, 'the figure of Edith Cavell is a beautiful conception, finely executed, but it is overshadowed and dwarfed by the great mass of granite which forms the background; and the squat figure representing Humanity, surmounting it, is as unpleasing as it is curious'.

British propaganda poster depicting the German 'murder' of Edith Cavell.

Edith Cavell is buried at Norwich cathedral and each October, on the anniversary of her death, a service of remembrance is held at her grave.

21 February 1916
The Start of the Battle of Verdun

As 1914 drew to a close, the Western Front had become a permanent fixture of trenches stretching 400 miles from the English Channel to Switzerland. Stalemate ensued. A year later, the situation was no better. Each side looked for a 'Big Push' that would break the opposing line of defence and bring about victory.

'France will bleed to death'

At the end of 1915, the German commander-in-chief, Erich von Falkenhayn, decided that Germany's 'arch enemy' was not France, but Britain. But to destroy Britain's will, Germany had first to defeat France. In a 'Christmas memorandum' to the German kaiser, Wilhelm II, Falkenhayn proposed an offensive that would compel the French to 'throw in every man they have. If they do so,' he continued, 'the forces of France will bleed to death'. The place to do this, Falkenhayn declared, would be Verdun.

An ancient town, Verdun in northeastern France, was, in 1915, surrounded by a string of sixty interlocked and reinforced forts. On 21 February 1916, the Battle of Verdun began. 1,200 German guns lined over only eight miles pounded the city which, despite intelligence warning of the impending attack, remained poorly defended. Verdun, which held a symbolic tradition among the French, was deemed not so important by the upper echelon of France's military. Joseph Joffre, the French commander, was slow to respond until the exasperated French prime minister, Aristide Briand, paid a night-time visit. Waking Joffre from his slumber, Briand insisted that he take the situation more seriously: 'You may not think losing Verdun a defeat – but everyone else will'.

'They shall not pass'

Galvanised into action, Joffre dispatched his top general, Henri-Philippe Pétain, to organise a stern defence of the city. Pétain managed to protect the only road leading into the city that remained open to the French. Every day, while under continuous fire, 2,000 lorries made a return trip along the 45-mile *Voie Sacrée* ('Sacred Way') bringing in vital supplies and reinforcements to be fed into the furnace that had become Verdun. Serving under Pétain was General Robert Nivelle who famously promised that the Germans *on ne passe pas*, 'they shall not pass', a quote often attributed to Pétain.

But the French were suffering grievous losses. Joffre demanded that his British counterpart, Sir Douglas Haig, open up the new offensive on the Somme, to the south of Verdun, to take the pressure of his beleaguered men. Haig, concerned that the new recruits to the British Army were not yet battle-ready, offered 15 August 1916 as a start date.

Joffre responded angrily that the French army would 'cease to exist' by then. Haig brought forward the offer to 1 July.

During June 1916, the attack and counterattack at Verdun continued. On the Eastern Front, the Russians attacked the Austrians, who, in turn, appealed to the Germans for help. Falkenhayn responded by calling a temporary halt at Verdun and transferring men east to aid the Austrians.

The Battle of Verdun wound down, then fizzled out entirely, officially ending on 18 December 1916. The French, under the stewardship of Generals Pétain and Nivelle regained much of what they had lost. After ten months of fighting, the city had been flattened, and the Germans and French, between them, had lost 260,000 men – one death for every 90 seconds of the battle. Men on all sides were bled to death but ultimately, Falkenhayn's big push achieved nothing.

5 June 1916
The Death of Lord Kitchener

Field Marshal Lord Kitchener's face and pointing finger proclaiming 'Your country needs you', often copied and mimicked, is one of the most recognizable posters of all time.

Born 24 June 1850 in County Kerry, Ireland, Horatio Kitchener first saw active service with the French army during the Franco-Prussian War of 1870-71 and, a decade later, with the British Army during the occupation of Egypt. He was part of the force that tried, unsuccessfully, to relieve General Charles Gordon, besieged in Khartoum in 1885. The death of Gordon, at the hands of Mahdist forces, caused great anguish in Britain. Thirteen years later, as commander-in-chief of the Egyptian army, Kitchener led the campaign of reprisal into the Sudan, defeating the Mahdists at the Battle of Omdurman and reoccupying Khartoum in 1898. Kitchener had restored Britain's pride.

Boer War

Kitchener's reputation took a dent however during the Second Boer War in South Africa, 1899-1902. Succeeding

Lord Roberts as commander-in-chief in November 1900 with the idea of mopping up outstanding pockets of resistance, Kitchener resorted to a scorched-earth policy in order to defeat the guerrilla tactics of the Boers. Controversially, he also set up a system of concentration camps and interned Boer women and children and black Africans. Overcrowded, lacking hygiene and malnourished, over 25,000 were to die, for which Kitchener was heavily criticised.

The criticism however, did not damage Kitchener's career, becoming first commander-in-chief of India, promoted to field marshal, and, in 1911, Consul-General of Egypt, responsible, in effect, for governing the whole country.

'Your country needs you'

At the outbreak of the First World War in 1914, Lord Kitchener was appointed Secretary of State for War, the first soldier to hold the post, serving under Herbert Asquith's Liberal government. Bleakly, he predicted a long war, a lone voice among the government and military elite who anticipated a short, sharp conflict. Britain, Kitchener argued, would need an army far larger than the existing 1914 professional army, the British Expeditionary Force (BEF). But the British, unlike their European counterparts, were against conscription. The answer was to raise an army of volunteers thus Kitchener went on a recruitment drive. From 7 August 1914, Kitchener's poster appeared across the country. The government hoped for perhaps 100,000 volunteers within the first six months. Any more would cause logistical problems. In the event, they got two million by the end of 1915, such was the extent of British patriotism and British naivety.

'A great poster'

Popular with the public but less so with the government, who found him taciturn and difficult to work with, the failure of the Gallipoli campaign saw Kitchener's prestige fall. In December 1915, Lord Kitchener suffered a demotion. He had offered to resign, but the government, knowing how popular he was with the public, daren't let him go. The prime minister's wife, Lady Margot Asquith, once famously said, 'if Kitchener was not a great man, he was, at least, a great poster.' (Although Lady Asquith later assigned the quote to her daughter). Kitchener's successor as secretary for war and eventual prime minister, David Lloyd George, thought little of Kitchener and criticised his wartime role in his 1937 *War Memoirs*. (Field Marshal Douglas Haig, Britain's commander-in-chief from December 1915, was another victim of Lloyd George's post-war denunciations).

In June 1916, Lord Kitchener was sent on a diplomatic mission to Russia to try and better coordinate the Western and Eastern Fronts. On 5 June, the ship he was travelling on, the armoured cruiser, HMS *Hampshire*, hit a German mine off the Orkney Islands and sunk. Nearly all drowned. Kitchener's body was never found, leading to several conspiracy theories that he had become too much of an embarrassment and liability, and had been assassinated. That David Lloyd George, at the time the Minister for Munitions, was supposed to have been accompanying Kitchener but cancelled at the last minute, merely added to the speculation. The editor of the *Manchester Guardian* remarked that Kitchener 'could not have done better than to have gone down, as he was a great impediment lately'.

Lord Kitchener's death shocked the nation and he was deeply mourned. But today, almost a century on from his death, his poster remains one of the iconic images of the twentieth century.

1 July 1916
The First Day of the Battle of the Somme

Within the collective British and Commonwealth psyche, no battle epitomises the futility of war as much as the Battle of the Somme. Almost 20,000 men were killed on the first day, 1 July 1916, alone.

German soldier at the Battle of the Somme, 1916.
German Federal Archives.

It started with the usual preliminary bombardment. Lasting five days, and involving 1,350 guns and 52,000 tonnes of explosives fired onto the German lines, British soldiers were assured that the 18-mile German frontline would be flattened – it would just be a matter of strolling across and taking possession of the German trenches.

The Battle of the Somme was designed to relieve the pressure on the French suffering at Verdun. The British army at the Somme consisted mainly of Kitchener recruits. Most had received only minimal training and many had still to grasp the skill of shooting accurately.

Dead men cannot move on

At 7.20 am on Saturday 1 July 1916 (a 'lovely, intensely hot day', according to one diarist), the first of seventeen mines was detonated; a huge explosion on the German lines at Hawthorn Ridge. The explosion was captured on film by official war photographer Geoffrey Malins and the Hawthorn Crater is still visible today.

The advance started ten minutes later, at seven thirty a.m. The massive explosions certainly alerted the German defenders of what was about to come.

To the right of the British, a smaller French force, transferred from the Battle of Verdun. As ordered, the men advanced in rigid lines. The bombardment combined with heavy rain the previous days had ensured that the ground was akin to a sea of mud and many an advancing soldier, lumbered with almost 70 lbs of equipment, drowned.

Re-enactment of Canadian troops 'going over the top', Battle of the Somme, 1916. Imperial War Museum.

Far from being decimated by the artillery, the German trenches ahead were brimming with guns pointing towards the advance. What followed went down as the worse day in British military history – 57,000 men fell on that first day alone, 19,240 of them dead. In return, the Germans suffered 185 casualties that first day. The Royal Newfoundland Regiment, for example, suffered ninety percent casualties – of the 780 Newfoundlanders that advanced on 1 July, only sixty-eight were available for duty the following day.

One of Britain's generals at the Battle of the Somme, Sir Beauvoir de Lisle, wrote, 'It was a remarkable display of training and discipline, and the attack failed only because dead men cannot move on'. Despite the appalling losses, Britain's commander-in-chief, Field Marshal Douglas Haig, decided to 'press [the enemy] hard with the least possible delay'. Thus the attack was resumed the following day.

And the day after that.

Cavalry and tanks

On 14 July, following a partially successful night-time attack, the British sent in the cavalry – a rare sight on the Western Front of World War One and one that stirred the romantic notions in old timers such as Haig. But the horses became bogged down in the mud, the Germans opened fire and few survived, either horse or man.

On 15 September, Haig introduced the modern equivalent of the cavalry onto the battlefield – the 'landship'. Originated in Britain, and championed by Winston Churchill, the designers tried to disguise them as water storage tanks giving them the codename 'tanks'. The name stuck. Despite advice to wait for more testing, Haig had insisted on their use at the Somme. He got his way and the introduction of 36 'Mark I', thirty ton tanks with a top speed of five mph, met with mixed results – many broke down but a few managed to penetrate German lines, 'frightening the Jerries out of their wits and making them scuttle like frightened rabbits', as one witness described it.

But, as always, the Germans soon plugged the hole forged by the tanks. Nonetheless, Haig was impressed and immediately ordered a thousand more. One witness described three of these 'huge mechanical monsters' firing on its own trench. 'Giving no thought to his own personal safety as he saw the tanks firing on his own men, the colonel ran forward and furiously rained blows with his cane on the side of one of the tanks.'

The Battle of the Somme ground on for a further two months. Nine Victoria Crosses were awarded on the first day alone; another 41 by the end of the battle. Soldiers from every part of the Empire were thrown into the melee – Australian, Canadian, New Zealanders, Indian and South African all took their part. The battle finally terminated on 18 November, after one hundred and forty days of fighting. 400,000 British and Commonwealth lives were lost, 200,000 French and 400,000 German. For this the Allies gained five miles. The Germans, having been pushed back, merely bolstered the already heavily-fortified second line, the Hindenburg Line.

As AJP Taylor put it in his *First World War*, first published in 1963, 'Idealism perished at the Battle of the Somme. The enthusiastic volunteers were enthusiastic no longer'.

Douglas Haig

Douglas Haig, Britain's First World War commander-in-chief from December 1915 to the end of the war, is remembered as the archetypal 'donkey' leading 'lions' to their death by the thousands. But, a century on, is this a fair judgment?

Born in Edinburgh, 19 June 1861, Douglas Haig was the eleventh son of a wealthy whiskey distiller. An expert horseman, he once represented England at polo. In 1898, he joined the forces of Lord Kitchener in the Sudan and, the following year, he served under Sir John French in Kitchener's army during the Boer War.

During the first year of the First World War, Haig served as a deputy to John French, the commander-in-chief of the British Expeditionary Force. Haig's actions at the Battle of Mons and the First Battle of Ypres earned him praise while, conversely, John French's fortunes plummeted following the Battle of Loos. Haig contributed to the drive to have the mood-swinging French removed and, in turn, in December 1915, was appointed by Prime Minister Herbert Asquith as French's replacement.

Douglas Haig, c1913. Library of Congress.

Cavalry man

A Presbyterian and firmly believing that God was on his side and therefore his decisions had to be right, Haig insisted on full frontal attacks, convinced that victory would come by military might alone. Still a cavalry man at heart, he believed the machine gun to be a 'much overrated weapon'. It is one of the criticisms levelled at Haig – that he was adverse to new technology. The evidence is contradictory. Almost a decade after the war, Haig still believed in the use of cavalry: *'I believe that the value of the horse and the opportunity for the horse in the future are likely to be as great as ever. Aeroplanes and tanks are only accessories to the men and the horse, and I feel sure that as time goes on you will find just as much use for the horse – the well-bred horse – as you have ever done in the past.'*

But Douglas Haig did back the introduction of the new 'landship', as the prototype tank was originally known. On 15 September 1916, during the Battle of the Somme, Haig ordered these new weapons onto the battlefield. Although many broke down, Haig was impressed enough to order a thousand more.

Butcher Haig?

Haig has often been criticized of being profligate of men's lives. His tenure as commander-in-chief saw the horrendous losses at the Battle of the Somme (July-November 1916) and the Third Battle of Ypres, otherwise known as Passchendaele, (July-November 1917). One private wrote, 'Haig's nickname was the butcher. He'd think nothing of sending thousands of men to certain death. The utter waste and disregard for human life and human suffering by the so-called educated classes who ran the country. What a wicked waste of life. I'd hate to be in their shoes when they face their Maker.'

David Lloyd George, prime minister of a coalition government from December 1916, had questioned the point of launching another costly offensive at Passchendaele but Haig had got the backing of the Conservatives within the coalition and so got his way. But Haig was often under pressure of his French allies to act, bringing forward, for example, the Somme offensive by six weeks to help take the pressure off the French at the long slug that was the Battle of Verdun. The question remains however would the extra six weeks to prepare made a difference? – the answer is probably not.

Historian, Basil Henry Liddell Hart, who fought during the war, described Haig as 'not merely immoral but criminal'. Yet the very nature of warfare during 1914-1918 meant that offence was no match against deeply entrenched defence. Haig was not alone – generals on all sides puzzled over this uncomfortable truth.

While Douglas Haig is remembered for the losses at the Somme and Passchendaele, it is often forgotten that from August 1918, he oversaw Britain's advance during what became known as the Hundred Days Offensive, the Allies' great push, in partnership with the overall Allied commander, the French commander-in-chief, Ferdinand Foch. The offensive ultimately led to victory and the surrender of the Germans on 11 November.

A land fit for heroes

Despite having a personal rapport with the king, George V, Haig never enjoyed the confidence of Lloyd George, who was openly critical of Haig's cavalier attitude with his men's lives. Lloyd George, in his *War Memoirs*, published in 1936, accused Haig of being 'second rate'. 'When he had to fight battles in quagmires he had never seen and over an area extending to a hundred miles which he never did or could personally inspect, he was lost.'

But by then Haig was dead and unable to defend himself.

It was Lloyd George, who during the election campaign of 1918, had promised a land 'fit for heroes to live in'. But it was Haig who did much to help veterans. In 1921, Haig was one of the founders of the Royal British

Legion, becoming its first president, a post he held until his death, and helped introduce the poppy of remembrance into Britain. He championed the rights of ex-servicemen and refused all state honours until the government improved their pensions, which duly came in August 1919. (Only then did Haig accept an earldom).

On 29 January 1928, Douglas Haig died from a heart attack brought on, according to his widow, by the strain of wartime command. He was sixty-six.

Haig's reticence certainly didn't help his own cause – prone to long silences and often coming across as callous. One journalist at the time described him as 'shy as a schoolgirl'. But at war's end, Haig was hailed as a hero, and his death saw much public grief, especially in his hometown of Edinburgh, and London, where up to a million people turned out to pay their respects.

Beastly attitudes

Haig's only son, Dawyck Haig, who was imprisoned in Colditz during the Second World War and who died in 2009, was a staunch defender of his father. In an interview to the BBC in June 2006, the eve of the 90th anniversary of the first day of the Somme, he said, 'He was not a brutish man, he was a very kind, wonderful man and by God, I miss him… I believe it has now turned full circle and people appreciate his contribution. But it saddens me my three sisters have not survived to see it. They died suffering from the beastly attitudes of the public towards our father.'

In 1937, a bronze statue of Douglas Haig, the Earl Haig Memorial, was unveiled on London's Whitehall.

Designed by sculptor, Alfred Frank Hardiman, and eight years in the making, it won many plaudits and prizes but unfortunately, the stance of the horse is that of one in the process of urinating.

The Douglas Haig statue, Whitehall, London.

15 October 1917
The Execution of Mata Hari

She enticed audiences with her dancing, her exoticism and eroticism – and her bejewelled bra, but in 1917, Mata Hari, a Malayan term meaning 'eye of the day', was shot by firing squad.

Margaretha Zelle

Born 7 August 1876 to a wealthy Dutch family, Margaretha Geertruida Zelle responded to a newspaper advertisement from a Rudolf MacLeod, a Dutch army officer of Scottish descent, seeking a wife. The pair married within three months of meeting each other and in 1895 moved to the Dutch East Indies (Indonesia) where they had two children.

The marriage was doomed from the beginning – twenty-two years older, MacLeod was an abusive husband and Zelle was never going to play the part of the dutiful wife. Their son died aged two from syphilis, reputably inherited from his father (their daughter would die a similar death, aged twenty-one) and in 1902, on their return to the Netherlands, they separated.

Unable to find work and uncertain about her future,

Zelle moved to Paris and there changed her name to Mata Hari, claiming she originated from India and was the daughter of a temple dancer. She started to earn a living by modelling and dancing, and found work in a cabaret. Exotically dressed, she became a huge success and was feted by the powerful and rich of Paris, taking on a number of influential lovers. She travelled numerous times between France and the Netherlands. But by now war had broken out and Mata Hari's movements and high-ranking liaisons caused suspicion.

Arrested

Arrested by the British, Hari was interrogated. She admitted to passing German information on to the French. In turn, the French discovered evidence, albeit of doubtful authenticity, that she was spying for the Germans under the codename 'H21'. Hari had indeed been recruited by the Germans, given the name H21 and received 20,000 francs as a down payment. Never one to turn down money, she accepted it but did no spying in return nor ever felt obliged to.

Returning to Paris, Hari was then arrested by the French and accused of being a double agent. The evidence against her was virtually non-existent, and the prosecution found not a single item or piece of information passed from Mata Hari to the Germans. The trial itself was of dubious nature as her defence was prohibited from cross-examining witnesses. Her defence lawyer was a seventy-four-year-old man, a former lover, and his association with Hari diminished his authority and the six-man jury had little hesitation in finding Mata Hari guilty.

And shot

At dawn on 15 October 1917, Mata Hari, wearing a three-cornered hat, was led out from her cell to face her death. She told an attendant nun, 'Do not be afraid, sister, I know how to die.' She refused to be tied to the stake or blindfolded, and waved at onlookers and blew kisses at the priest and her lawyer. She was shot by a 12-man firing squad, each wearing a red fez. The officer in charge ensured she was dead by firing a bullet into her head. She was forty-one.

Thirty years later, one of the prosecutors admitted that 'there wasn't enough evidence [against Mata Hari] to flog a cat.'

Winston Churchill and the First World War

Winston Churchill rather enjoyed war. In July 1914, as Britain prepared for the oncoming catastrophe, Churchill, at the time the First Lord of the Admiralty, wrote to his wife, 'I am interested, geared up and happy. Is it not horrible to be built like that?' And in 1916, in a letter to David Lloyd George's daughter, Churchill admitted: 'I think a curse should rest on me — because I love this war. I know it's smashing and shattering the lives of thousands every moment, and yet, I can't help it, I enjoy every second of it'.

Churchill had been appointed to the Admiralty in October 1911, and had continued the policy established by his predecessor of keeping Britain ahead of the Germans and strengthening the navy by expanding the number of Dreadnoughts, the most powerful battleship of the time.

But despite these preparations, Britain suffered a number of setbacks during the first months of the First World War – on 22 September 1914, the German navy sunk a number of British ships at Dogger Bank (sixty miles off the east coast of England in the North Sea), killing 1,459 sailors; and on 16 December, German ships penetrated close enough to British shores to attack Scarborough, Hartlepool and Whitby causing 137 fatalities. Churchill, in his role at the Admiralty, took the brunt of the blame and the public's anger.

Winston Churchill, 1904. Imperial War Museum.

Antwerp

In October 1914, with German forces bearing down on Antwerp, the British government dispatched Churchill to Belgium. Although, through his efforts, he helped delay the fall of the city by about a week, allowing the Belgian Army to escape and the vital Channel ports to be saved, he was still heavily criticised at home for failing to save the city.

Stung by the criticism, Churchill offered to resign

from the government in return for a post as an army officer in the field. His offer, met with derision and loud guffaws, was refused.

The Landship

Throughout the war, Churchill furthered the cause of the newly-developed 'landships', or, to use its original code word, the 'tank'. On 15 September 1916, during the Battle of the Somme, the British commander-in-chief, Sir Douglas Haig, introduced the tank, the modern equivalent of the cavalry, onto the battlefield.

Gallipoli

In 1915, the British planned to use the Royal Navy to take control of the Dardanelles Straits from where they could attack Constantinople, the capital of the Ottoman Empire. The Dardanelles, a strait of water separating mainland Turkey and the Gallipoli peninsula, is sixty miles long and, at its widest, only 3.5 miles.

As First Lord of the Admiralty, Churchill insisted that the Royal Navy, acting alone, could succeed. On 19 February, a flotilla of British and French ships pounded the outer forts of the Dardanelles and a month later attempted to penetrate the strait. It failed, losing six ships, half its fleet. Soldiers, it was decided, would be needed after all, and Horatio Kitchener was called in.

Finally, in January 1916, after the loss of some 220,000 Allied casualties, the curtain fell on the whole sorry 'side show' that was Gallipoli. Although Churchill's responsibility in Gallipoli had, by and large, ceased once the army had been deployed, he was still much criticised for his involvement, and the disaster at Gallipoli was a severe setback to Churchill's reputation. Indeed, his wife, Clementine, said that 'the Dardanelles haunted [Churchill] for the rest of his life. I thought he'd never get over the Dardanelles. I thought he would die of grief.'

The humiliation of Gallipoli, together with a scandal about the supply of shells, forced the Liberal prime minister, Herbert Asquith, to form a coalition government. One of the conditions, as laid down by the Conservatives, was that Churchill, a Liberal, be relieved of his cabinet duties. He was. Appointed to the rather meaningless post of Chancellor of the Duchy of Lancaster, Churchill bemoaned, 'I am finished'.

Lieutenant Colonel

Demoted and demoralised, Churchill handed in his resignation from the coalition government and, although he remained an MP, joined the frontline troops as a lieutenant colonel of the Royal Scot Fusiliers on the Western Front. By all accounts, although unorthodox as an officer, he was popular and courageous, and improved morale by organising entertainment for the troops and reducing punishments.

In January 1916, his battalion moved onto the front line. Although he spent only about a hundred days at the front, Churchill led by example, venturing thirty times or so into no man's land, often flirting with death. His comrades noticed he never ducked while at the front. But, as Churchill said, 'It's no damn use ducking. The bullet has gone a long way past you by now!'

In March 1916, Churchill, eager to get back to politics, resigned his army commission and returned to London. But things did not go according to plan. In December 1916, Asquith was replaced as the coalition's prime minister by David Lloyd George but there was still no position for the eager Churchill. Lloyd George's welcome was not one to lift his hopes, writing to Churchill: 'You do not win trust even where you command admiration'.

Finally, in July 1917, despite protests and strong vocal disproval from the Conservatives, Churchill was appointed Minister of Munitions but it was still a post outside the cabinet and his duties there were mainly administrative.

Winston Churchill as Minister of Munitions meeting workers near Glasgow, 9 October 1918. Imperial War Museum.

Red Peril

In January 1919, following the end of the war, Churchill

was appointed Secretary of State for War and Secretary of State for Air.

Deeply alarmed by the Bolshevik threat, the 'red peril', following the Russian Revolution and the downfall of the tsar, Churchill poured troops into Russia to assist the counter-revolutionary cause during the Russian Civil War. 'The foul baboonery of Bolshevism', as he called it, must be 'strangled in its cradle'. Churchill was concerned lest Bolshevism should spread to Germany and so urged his colleagues at the Paris Peace Conference to treat Germany as friends in the post-war world: 'Kill the Bolshie, Kiss the Hun,' as he wrote to Violet Asquith.

But the Bolsheviks survived and, following the defeat of the 'Whites', the last remaining British troops were withdrawn in 1920.

Inter-war

Losing his seat as a Liberal MP, Churchill swapped sides and served a Conservative government as Chancellor of the Exchequer until their defeat in the election of 1929. Although the Conservatives were re-elected in 1931, Churchill, considered too much a loose canon, was sidelined – again. He remained in the shadows throughout the thirties, writing and painting, until recalled to the Admiralty in 1939, by which time the Second World War had begun.

10 November 1918
The Abdication of Kaiser Wilhelm II

The Kaiser would 'like every day to be his birthday' was Otto von Bismarck's damning assessment of Wilhelm II.

Hot head

Wilhelm II, Tsar Nicholas II of Russia and King George V of Britain were all cousins. George and Wilhelm were both grandsons of Queen Victoria, and Nicholas's wife, the Empress Alexandra, was Victoria's granddaughter. They met, as a threesome, only twice. Winston Churchill described Wilhelm as a 'very ordinary, vain but on the whole a well-meaning man'. Queen Victoria's judgment was somewhat harsher, calling her grandson 'such a hot-headed, conceited and wrong-headed young man'.

Like a victim of unrequited love, Wilhelm loved the English and hated and resented them at the same time. In 1889, Grandmother Victoria made Wilhelm an honorary admiral of the Royal Navy. Gushing with thanks, Wilhelm promised he would always take an interest in Britain's fleet as if it was his own. He had a chest made of oak from Nelson's *Victory*.

Kaiser Wilhelm II, 1902. Imperial War Museum.

Born on 27 January 1859 with a paralyzed left arm, considerably shorter than the right, Wilhelm needed help with eating and dressing throughout his life, and went to great lengths to hide his disability. He had, for example, a specially-made fork to help him with his food. He owned over 30 castles throughout Germany and would visit them all occasionally, indulging in socialising and hunting – he was capable of killing a thousand or more animals in the course of a weekend's hunt.

Wilhelm loved all things military. He reputably owned some 600 uniforms, many he designed himself. But his military knowledge was superficial at best and as the war progressed, he was increasingly side-lined by his generals. His knowledge of political matters was equally shallow, having neither the enthusiasm nor attention span to read lengthy or detailed reports.

Wilhelm's power, he firmly believed, was God-given. Any criticism of him or his policies was, in effect, an act of blasphemy. Germany, he said, 'must follow me wherever I go.'

Britain's foreign secretary, Sir Edward Grey, once said of the Kaiser, 'The German Emperor is like a battleship with steam up and screws going, but with no rudder, and he will run into something some day and cause a catastrophe. He has the strongest army in the world and the Germans don't like being laughed at and are looking for somebody on whom to vent their temper and use their strength. It is thirty-eight years since Germany had her last war, and she is very strong and very restless, like a person whose boots are too small for him.'

The Kaiser's War

The assassination of Archduke Franz Ferdinand on 28 June 1914 by Gavrilo Princip, a member of a Serbian terrorist group, had given Austria-Hungary the opportunity to assert its authority over Serbia. But first it sought reassurance from its powerful ally, Germany. Wilhelm II gave Austria-Hungary the assurance it needed then promptly went off on a cruise around Norway. By the time he returned from holiday, the whole of Europe was teetering on the edge of war.

In late 1918, with the tide of war turning against Germany, the Kaiser's generals, especially Erich

Ludendorff, were tempted by US president Woodrow Wilson's Fourteen Points – a blueprint for a post-war peace that would have avoided overly-punitive terms on a vanquished Germany. But Wilson was demanding democracy in Germany. On 3 October, on Ludendorff's urging, Wilhelm appointed the liberal Prince Maximilian of Baden chancellor of Germany. But Wilhelm's nod towards parliamentary democracy was not enough for the US president – he demanded the Kaiser's abdication.

In November 1918, Paul von Hindenburg and Wilhelm Groener (Ludendorff's replacement) went to see Wilhelm, who had bolted to army headquarters in the Belgium town of Spa. Hindenburg, a monarchist, bowed his head in shame and left Groener to do the talking.

Wilhelm remained defiant until the news came through – in Berlin, Prince Max had proclaimed a socialist republic – the new Germany had no room for a monarch. Thus, on 10 November, Kaiser Wilhelm II abdicated. The five hundred-year rule of the Hohenzollern dynasty had come to an end. Wilhelm fled to the Netherlands and into exile, never again to step on German soil.

The following day at five a.m., Paris time, the Western Front armistice was signed and came into effect six hours later at eleven a.m. War was over.

Exile

Following the war and his forced abdication, the ex-kaiser lived in exile in the Dutch town of Doorn. King George V described his cousin as 'the greatest criminal in history'. The Dutch queen, Queen Wilhelmina, declined ever to meet the fallen kaiser but when the Paris Peace

Conference requested Wilhelm's extradition to face trial for war crimes, she refused to hand him over.

Wilhelm II in exile, Doorn, 1933. German Federal Archives.

In 1940, with Hitler's armies bearing down on the Netherlands, the Dutch royal family fled to Britain. Wilhelm however did not, even refusing Winston Churchill's offer of asylum. In fact, Wilhelm rather admired what Hitler was doing and supported the 'elimination of the British and the Jews' from Europe, adding, 'The Jews [are] being thrust out of their nefarious positions in all countries'. Following the fall of France in June 1940, Wilhelm sent Hitler a telegram in which he wrote, 'Congratulations, you have won using *my* troops'. Hitler was unimpressed.

Wilhelm was content to continue living in occupied Holland, believing that the Nazis would restore the monarchy and the kaiser to his throne. Of course they did not, and the eighty-two-year-old embittered private citizen, once a kaiser, died the following year on 4 June 1941. Hitler, despite his animosity towards Wilhelm, wanted to give the old kaiser a state funeral in Berlin but was unable to override Wilhelm's wishes that his body should not be returned to Germany until the monarchy was restored. However, another of Wilhelm's stipulations, that there should be no Nazi regalia at his funeral, was ignored and his funeral was adorned with swastikas.

Georges Clemenceau

Nicknamed the Tiger for his fiery temperament, French prime minister, Georges Clemenceau, was not averse to settling personal feuds by duel. He was anti-monarchy, anti-socialist and anti-Catholic. His father, Benjamin, who himself had been imprisoned for his republican views, was a doctor and although Clemenceau completed his medical studies, he didn't take up the profession, being drawn instead to politics.

A staunch republican and troublemaker, like his father, Georges Clemenceau was once imprisoned for seventy-three days (some sources state seventy-seven days) by Napoleon III's government for publishing a republican newspaper and trying to incite demonstrations against the monarchy. In 1865, fearing another arrest, and possible incarceration on Devil's Island, Clemenceau fled to the US, arriving in 1865, towards the end of the American Civil War. He lived first in New York, where he worked as a journalist, and then in Connecticut where he became a teacher in a private girls' school. Clemenceau married one of his American students, Mary Plummer, and together they had three children before divorcing seven years later. (Of his son, Clemenceau, known for his wit, said, 'If he had not become a Communist at twenty-two, I would have disowned him. If he is still a Communist at thirty, I will do it then.')

Five days after his divorce, Clemenceau returned to France and briefly worked as a doctor before returning to politics. In 1871, he witnessed France's defeat to Prussia in the Franco-Prussian War.

A soldier of democracy

An intellectual, Georges Clemenceau was fascinated by Ancient Greek culture, supported the work of the French Impressionists, wrote a book on Jewish history, and translated into French the works of English philosopher, John Stuart Mill. Following France's defeat during the Franco-Prussian War, Clemenceau opposed France's colonial ambitions, arguing that the country needed to concentrate its efforts on extracting revenge on the Germans and recovering Alsace Lorraine, territory it had lost to the Germans as part of the French surrender.

In March 1906, Clemenceau was appointed Home Affairs Minister where he earned his 'tiger' nickname and gained a reputation as a fierce opponent of socialism and the trade unions, most famously, in May 1906, sending in the military to suppress a miners' strike. From October 1906 until July 1909, Clemenceau served his first term as prime minister.

Having been ousted from power, Clemenceau travelled across South America advocating the benefits of democracy: 'I am a soldier of democracy. It is the only form of government which can establish equality for all, and which can bring closer the ultimate goals: freedom and justice.'

'I wage war'

During the early part of the First World War, Clemenceau, refusing a position within the government, became a vocal critic of France's strategy, especially that of Joseph Joffre, chief of the French army. However, in November 1917, aged seventy-six, he was appointed, for a second term, as prime minister, leading a coalition government and overseeing France's role in the eventual defeat of Germany. (He also concurrently served as the Minister for War).

On returning to power, he promised, 'No more pacifist campaigns, no more German intrigues. Neither treason, nor semi-treason: the war. Nothing but the war.' He cracked down on all dissenters and doomsayers within France, authorised the execution of spies and traitors, most notoriously Mata Hari, and, in the words of Britain's wartime prime minister, David Lloyd George, 'possessed restless energy and indomitable courage'. He paid frequent visits to the trenches, helped improve the morale of the French troops and became known, affectionately, as 'Father of Victory'. In March 1918, he famously said, 'My home policy: I wage war. My foreign policy: I wage war. All the time I wage war.'

Versailles

In the subsequent post-war Paris Peace Conference, Georges Clemenceau found it 'far easier to make war than peace'. He took a firm line, determined to see Germany crippled to prevent it from ever again becoming a military threat, but Britain and the US (represented by US president, Woodrow Wilson) were against such harsh measures, believing it vital to Europe's future wellbeing that Germany be made stable. Lloyd George believed that Clemenceau's proposals would 'plunge Germany and the greater part of Europe into Bolshevism.' Nonetheless, Clemenceau scored a symbolic victory – at his insistence, the Treaty of Versailles was signed in the Hall of Mirrors at the Palace of Versailles where, in 1871, the French had surrendered to the Germans.

On 19 February 1919, during the conference, Clemenceau survived an assassination attempt. His assailant fired from close range and one bullet, which hit the prime minister in the ribs, remained there for the rest of his life. Clemenceau joked that, 'We have just won the most terrible war in history, yet here is a Frenchman who misses his target six out of seven times at point-blank range… I suggest that he be locked up for eight years, with intensive training in a shooting gallery.'

Although Clemenceau managed to negotiate Alsace Lorraine's return to France, he had to compromise on too many points and he left the conference feeling that Germany had been dealt with too lightly. The French public agreed and took out their frustrations on Clemenceau. Dissatisfied with their prime minister's performance at Versailles, he was voted out of office in the elections of January 1920.

Finally, at the age of 80, the old tiger was able to retire. In his latter years, Clemenceau warned against a resurgent Germany, predicting a new war by 1940.

Georges Clemenceau died, aged eighty-eight, at home in Paris on 24 November 1929.

World War One Memorial Plaques

In October 1916, the British government decided to award a token of commemoration for the next of kin to those that had fallen in the war while serving Great Britain and her empire. They settled on a bronze plaque and set up a competition to design it. Judges included directors of London's Victoria and Albert Museum and National Gallery. The competition generated such interest that the deadline had to be extended to 31 December 1917. In the event, the judges received over 800 designs.

Three months later, they announced a shortlist of seven in *The Times*, each of which was put on public display at the V&A. From these seven, the winner was chosen – a design by thirty-two-year-old, Edward Carter Preston. Mr Carter Preston's design was that of Britannia aside a lion, holding a laurel wreath in one hand and a trident in the other. Beneath her is another lion gorging the German eagle, and the two dolphins are meant to represent Britain's sea power. The inscription reads '*He died for freedom and honour*' and a space was left for the fallen's name but not his / her rank – in death all soldiers and servicemen and women are equal in the eyes of God, regardless of rank.

A Brave Life

Production of the memorial plaques did not begin until December 1918, a month after the war's end. About 1,300,000 were produced, of which six hundred commemorated women. The families of the three hundred and six British servicemen executed during the war did not receive the plaque.

Families received their plaques together with an embossed letter from the king, George V, with the following words:

> *I join my grateful people in sending you this memorial of a brave life given for others in the Great War.*
> *George R.I.*

The Treaty of Versailles

On 28 June 1919, Germany reluctantly signed the Treaty of Versailles as part of the Paris Peace Conference in the Hall of Mirrors at the Palace of Versailles – exactly five years on from the assassination of Archduke Franz Ferdinand, the spark that had ignited the First World War.

On being presented with the document, in early June,

Germany was given three weeks to comply. The German government complained that having not been consulted, the terms of the Treaty of Versailles were nothing less than a dictate set by the representatives of the thirty-two nations present. (The conference was led by the Allies, the 'Big Four', represented by, pictured above left to right: David Lloyd George for Great Britain, Vittorio Orlando for Italy, Georges Clemenceau for France and Woodrow Wilson for the US). Germany had not been permitted to take part in the talks and ultimately the German government was too weak, both politically and militarily, to do anything but add its signature, which, on 28 June, they duly did.

The Treaty of Versailles was only one of five treaties produced by the Paris Peace Conference, one for each of the defeated Central Powers, none of whom were in attendance, and each named after a Parisian suburb.

The Treaty of Sevres, for example, officially closed down the Ottoman Empire and virtually abolished Turkish sovereignty, while the Treaty of Trianon imposed strict punishments on Hungary.

The League of Nations

Out of the talks came the founding of the League of Nations, an international body to help maintain peace and arbitrate over disputes. The idea was originally Wilson's and formed part of his 'Fourteen Points', a blueprint he formulated in January 1918 for the future peace. The Paris Peace Conference was meant to provide the means to ensure that the Great War, as it was known then, was 'the war to end war', the phrase coined by HG Wells and often attributed to Wilson. But Lloyd George was more accurate when, mockingly, he said, 'This war, like the next war, is a war to end war'.

The Treaty of Versailles

The terms of the Treaty of Versailles were harsh and not for negotiation. Germany lost thirteen percent of her territory, which meant twelve percent of Germans now lived in a foreign country, and Germany's colonial possessions were redistributed among the other colonial powers. The German Rhineland, on the border with France, was to be demilitarized (stripped of an armed presence) and placed under Allied control until 1935. The small but industrially important Saar region was to be governed by Britain and France for fifteen years and its coal exported to France in recompense for the French coal mines destroyed by Germany during the war. After fifteen years a plebiscite (or referendum) of the Saar population would decide its future.

Most of West Prussia was given to Poland. The German city of Danzig (modern-day Gdansk) was made a 'free' city so that Poland could have use of a port. To give Poland access to Danzig, they were given a strip of land, the 'Polish Corridor', through Prussia, thereby cutting East Prussia off from the rest of Germany.

Militarily, Germany's army was to be limited to a token 100,000 men, and its navy to 15,000, plus a ban on conscription. She was not permitted to have an air force, nor tanks, and was prohibited from producing or importing weaponry.

The payment of reparations was for 'compensation

for all damage done to the civilian population of the Allied powers and their property'. It was to include raw material, such as the coal from the Saar and Ruhr regions. Two years later, in 1921, the cost of reparations was announced – £6.6 billion, which German economists calculated would take until 1988 to pay. The figure shocked and angered Germans who conveniently forgot that Germany had demanded an even greater sum from a defeated France following the Franco-Prussian War of 1870–1.

But it was the humiliating clause that forced Germany into accepting responsibility for the war and for the damage to the civilian populations of the Allies that rankled most with the public at home.

'An armistice for twenty years.'

Ultimately, the treaty satisfied no one. Britain thought it too harsh, believing an economically weak Germany would be detrimental to all Europe; Wilson returned to the US to find a country increasingly isolationist in its outlook and a Senate that refused to either ratify the treaty or join the League of Nations; and the French who felt it not harsh enough. It was they, the French argued, who had suffered most during the war. The French public was so dissatisfied with their prime minister, Clemenceau, that they voted him out six months later, replacing him with Ferdinand Foch who, with sharp intuition, said, 'This is not peace, this is an armistice for twenty years.'

Italy, lured into war in 1915 by territorial promises, was treated dismissively during talks causing its prime minister, Vittorio Orlando, to walk out. Italy was disappointed by its spoils of war. Orlando, heavily criticised by Italy's rising Right, led by Benito Mussolini, was soon ousted.

Germany was outraged by the Treaty of Versailles and Germans throughout the country rounded on the politicians that had signed it. The war had been lost, not by the German army, they claimed, but the politicians – the government had 'stabbed the nation in the back'. After all, not since 1914 had a single foreign soldier stepped on German soil. The new Weimar government, although democratically elected, was deemed responsible for Germany's humiliation, and criticized by all sides for its weakness in standing up to the Allies. In March 1920 the *Freikorps*, led by Wolfgang Kapp, tried to seize power in Berlin but the coup, unable to gain the army's support, failed.

The Kapp Putsch may have failed but there was another agitator waiting in the wings, seething at how Germany had been betrayed by its politicians. His name was Adolf Hitler.

Woodrow Wilson

Born 28 December 1856 in Virginia to a slave owning Presbyterian minister, Woodrow Wilson became the first Southerner to obtain the office of US president since Andrew Johnson, who's tenure ended in 1869.

A world safer for democracy

Elected the twenty-eighth US president in 1911, Woodrow Wilson, a Democrat, was determined to maintain American neutrality during the First World War. He was re-elected in 1916 on the slogan, 'He kept us out of the war'. But Germany's policy of unrestricted submarine warfare, which cost American lives, together with the exposure of the Zimmermann Telegram, forced the president's hand. Wilson sought and received Congress' mandate and on 6 April 1917, the US declared war on Germany, a course of action necessary, according to Wilson, to make the 'world safer for democracy'.

On 8 January 1918, in a speech to Congress, Wilson delivered his Fourteen Points, a programme for peace based on the principles of democracy and justice and not on punishment and reparations. Wilson hoped it would encourage the Germany to seek peace. Georges Clemenceau, the new French prime minister, was scathing of Wilson's Points – 'Fourteen? The good Lord only had ten'. The establishment of a body to act as an international arbitrator, the League of Nations, was also core to Wilson's philosophy.

As the autumn of 1918 progressed, and Germany's war was effectively lost, the German government was keen to accept Wilson's promise of non-punitive measures. But there was a price to pay – Wilson demanded that Germany appoint a parliament in its first steps towards democracy, and, most shockingly, he demanded the abdication of the Kaiser, Wilhelm II. The Kaiser duly abdicated on 10 November 1918 and went into exile in the Netherlands, never to step on German soil again. The following day, the armistice was signed, bringing to an end the First World War.

The war to end war

Wilson attended the Paris Peace Conference and, in doing so, became the first US president to travel to Europe while in office. By the time the conference finished in January 1920, little of Wilson's Fourteen Points remained and the terms imposed on Germany in the Treaty of Versailles were indeed punitive. The League of Nations however did become a reality. Wilson had used the phrase, 'the war to end war', originally coined by the writer HG Wells, and the existence and work of the League of Nations was to help prevent another war of such a scale. But Great Britain's prime minister, David Lloyd George, was more accurate when, mockingly, he said, 'This war, like the next war, is a war to end war'.

The League's inaugural assembly took place within a few days of the conference ending. Forty-two nations signed up for the League but the US was not one of them. During the twenty-six years of the League's existence, the US never joined.

New role and new responsibility

Wilson returned to America to find much opposition to the treaty both from isolationists and Republicans. On 10 July 1919, addressing the US Senate, Wilson urged US participation in the League, citing, 'a new role and a new responsibility have come to this great nation that we honor and which we would all wish to lift to yet higher levels of service and achievement'.

Despite receiving the Nobel Peace Prize in October 1919, Wilson had limited backing. While touring the nation, trying to garner support, Wilson suffered the first of several strokes.

Paralyzed on his left side and blind in one eye, Wilson effectively retired from his duties but remained in office until the election of November 1920.

Wilson's successor in the White House, Republican Warren Harding, neither allowed the US to join the League of Nations or ratify the Treaty of Versailles.

Woodrow Wilson died on 3 February 1924, aged sixty-seven. He is the only US president to be buried in Washington DC.

The League of Nations

Following the end of the First World War, US president, Woodrow Wilson, proposed a programme of Fourteen Points to be presented at the Paris Peace Conference. The fourteenth point suggested the formation of an international body to help maintain future peace and arbitrate over disputes. The exact wording was as follows:

'A general association of nations must be formed under specific covenants for the purpose of affording mutual guarantees of political independence and territorial integrity to great and small states alike.'

Endorsed by the peace conference, the League of Nations was founded on 28 June 1919, the day the Treaty of Versailles was signed, with forty-two founding members, and held its first meeting in Paris on 16 January 1920. Its HQ, however, was in Geneva and a British diplomat, Sir Eric Drummond, its first (of three) Secretary-General.

Member states came and went but sixty-three nations belonged to the League at one time or another, the most notable exception being the US. In 1919, an increasingly isolationist US refused to ratify the Treaty of Versailles and never joined the League of Nations as a member despite the efforts of Woodrow Wilson. For a brief five months period (September 1934 to February 1935) there was a record fifty-eight members.

Dogged

However the League was dogged almost from the start. Germany was admitted in 1926 and the Soviet Union in 1934. The League oversaw various mandates (particularly in Iraq, Palestine and Lebanon); supervised the free city of Danzig in Poland; managed to settle disputes between competing nations, notably between the Soviet Union and Poland in 1921, and dealt with the practicalities of child welfare and refugee movements.

Failures

But its failures were of greater significance. It failed to stop Japan from invading Manchuria in 1931 (despite both Japan and China being members); dealt inadequately with

Italy's invasion of Abyssinia in 1936, (also both members); and its influence was notably lacking following Hitler's invasion of Czechoslovakia in 1938.

Unlike the United Nations, the League never possessed a military wing so any punitive measures were limited to sanctions and harshly-worded but usually ineffectual missives.

Withdrawal

Hitler withdrew Germany from the League in 1933 and free of the League's (limited) interference was able to step-up Germany's rearmament programme. Japan also withdrew in 1933 and Italy in 1937.

In 1939, during the early months of World War Two, the Soviet Union, still a member, invaded fellow-member Finland, for which it was expelled from the League. It is unlikely that Joseph Stalin felt overly perturbed.

Its work during the war was restricted to humanitarian and practical ventures but politically the League was a spent-force.

On 18 April 1946, the League of Nations gave way to the United Nations.

Contacting the First World War dead – Arthur Conan Doyle and Spiritualism

It is almost midnight. The only light emanates from a few candles placed around the room. In the middle of the drawing room is a round table adorned only with a pale linen cloth. Around it sits a couple and a companion. The man is in his fifties, barrel-chested with a long moustache. He holds his wife's hands. The third person, a medium, rocks to and fro, her eyes tightly closed. She is mumbling in a high-pitched voice, groaning, breathing hard, but, frothing slightly from the mouth, her words are unintelligible. The couple watch her intently, waiting, hoping for a communication.

Suddenly it comes. Her tone changes. 'Jean, it is I,' she says in the voice of a young man.

Instantly, the couple recognise the voice. The woman, Jean, gasps, 'It is Kingsley.'

'Is that you, boy?' says the man, his hands tightening over his wife's.

Lowering his voice to a whisper, Kingsley says, 'Father, forgive me.'

The man's heart lurches, 'There was never anything to forgive. You were the best son a man ever had.'

He feels a hand on his head then a kiss just above his brow. It takes his breath away.

'Are you happy?' he cries.

There is a pause and then very gently, 'Yes, I am so happy.'

'Christianity is dead'

Contacting the dead was a popular pursuit post-First World War, when so many parents had lost loved ones in the killing fields of the Western Front, Gallipoli and further afield. The war was without precedent in terms of fatalities, and people, throughout Europe, haunted by a generation of slaughtered men, found themselves struggling for answers. The technology of warfare had defeated everything they previously held dear – and religion had failed to provide the answers. Instead, many turned to spiritualism as a means to contact their dead directly.

And the leading proponent for spiritualism was none other than Sir Arthur Conan Doyle. His greatest invention, the straight-laced Sherlock Holmes, would have thoroughly disapproved of his creator's conversion to séances, Ouija boards and mediums. But the great writer had lost his son, Kingsley, in October 1918, and like so many grief-struck parents, he was desperate to commune with his dead son from beyond the grave. 'Christianity is dead,' he once declared, 'How else could ten million young men have marched out to slaughter? Did any moral force stop that war? No. Christianity is dead – dead!'

Kingsley Conan Doyle had been wounded in the neck on the first day of the Battle of the Somme, 1 July 1916. 20,000 British soldiers were killed that day, plus another 40,000 wounded – the worst, single day in Britain's military history. Two years later, however, Kingsley was recovering. But in the summer of 1918, the whole world was swept by Spanish Flu, the most devastating pandemic in modern times, which claimed at least fifty million lives. Among them, on 28 October, was twenty-five-year-old Kingsley, his resistance compromised by his battlefield injury.

Four months later, the pandemic claimed Conan Doyle's brother, Innes. Conan Doyle fell into a deep depression but consoled by the fact he knew he could, at some point, reach out and contact them on the other side. But Conan Doyle's belief in spiritualism was not caused by his son and brother's deaths – it had been his firm conviction for many decades.

Born into a strict Roman Catholic family, Conan Doyle had all but lost his faith by the time he was seventeen. Declaring himself agnostic, he nonetheless felt an emptiness in his being. So, as a young newly-qualified doctor practicing in Southsea, near Portsmouth, he researched what he called 'new religions'. In 1880, the twenty-one-year-old doctor attended his first séance. It made a huge impression on him.

Seven years later, Conan Doyle published the first of a series that would make him a rich man and make his name the world over – *A Study in Scarlet*, starring Sherlock Holmes. But it was also in this same year, 1887, that Conan Doyle declared himself a spiritualist.

Conan Doyle formed a small group that met regularly in Southsea, trying their hand, with mixed results, at séances. But it was the appearance of a real medium, experienced at summoning the dead, that convinced Conan Doyle. 'After weighing the evidence,' he wrote, 'I could no more doubt the existence of the phenomena than I could doubt the existence of lions in Africa.'

The Death of Sherlock Holmes

Conan Doyle wrote more Sherlock Holmes and the pipe-smoking detective made him rich. But very soon Holmes, and his erstwhile companion, Dr Watson, was keeping Conan Doyle from what he really wanted to do. Writing to his mother, Conan Doyle said, '[Holmes] takes my mind from better things'. For Conan Doyle, 'better things' meant spiritualism. The death of Holmes was not long in coming. In 1893, only six years after his first appearance, Conan Doyle killed off his indomitable sleuth, drowning him in the Reichenbach Falls in the Swiss Alps.

Now, free of the demands of his detective, Conan Doyle was able to devote all his energies to spiritualism. But not for long. So outraged were his fans by the death of Sherlock Holmes, Conan Doyle had no choice but to bring him back to life, employing a literary sleight of hand. Sherlock Holmes was to remain his occasional and mostly unwelcome companion for the rest of his life.

In 1914, the Great War, as it was originally called, broke out. No war has been so associated with the paranormal as the First World War. The first and most notorious case occurred in August 1914. British forces had just been beaten by an advance of Germans near the Belgium town of Mons and were forced into a retreat. As the army retreated, British soldiers claimed they saw apparitions either in the form of angels or archers from the Battle of Agincourt, 1415, depending on who was telling the tale, that provided them safe passage.

Conan Doyle's brother-in-law and good friend, Malcolm Leckie, was killed at Mons. Together with his second wife, Jean, Conan Doyle immediately began trying to dredge Leckie up from the dead through a series of séances.

The Other Side

In 1916, with the war at its height, and still seeking answers, Conan Doyle stepped up his interest in spiritualism. Whereas before he had only 'dallied' with the subject, now he was prepared to embrace fully a 'breaking down of the walls between two worlds, a direct undeniable message from beyond, a call of hope and of guidance to the human race at the time of its deepest affliction'. Spiritualism was the answer to the world's problems.

Kingsley, a firm Christian, had had no truck with his father's spiritualism, which is why, when talking to him from the 'other side', he begged his father's forgiveness for having always doubted him.

Following the war, Sir and Lady Conan Doyle stepped up their campaign – they toured the country and journeyed to Australia and the US. With the energy and enthusiasm of committed converts, they embarked on a series of gruelling tours, proclaiming their message to huge audiences.

Many of his friends and contemporaries found him foolish, not least his friend, the American Harry Houdini, the famous escapologist and magician. Houdini, momentarily interested in spiritualism following the death of his mother, soon realised it was nothing but hoax and trickery, performed by mercenary conmen exploiting the bereaved and vulnerable. The two men went to great lengths to prove each other wrong to the point of falling out. Following Houdini's death in 1926, Conan Doyle hoped to settle it for once and all by summoning the magician from the dead. But Houdini, even from the other side, held to his guns.

The Cottingley Fairies

Conan Doyle's reputation was questioned even more when

he declared his utter belief in the Cottingley fairies. Two young girls, cousins, had used paper cut-outs of fairies and photographed themselves with them in their garden in the village of Cottingley in Yorkshire. By the time Conan Doyle, a great believer in fairies, was declaring the photos' authenticity to the world, even going so far to write a book on the subject, *The Coming of the Fairies*, the two young girls dared not say that it was no more than a silly prank.

Conan Doyle dutifully continued to write Sherlock Holmes; the last collection of short stories, *The Case-Book of Sherlock Holmes*, was published in 1927, three years before Conan Doyle's death. But despite the ridicule and the antagonism, Conan Doyle stuck to his spiritualist beliefs as he entered old age. In 1930, aged seventy-one, he wrote, 'The reader will judge that I have had many adventures. The greatest and most glorious of all awaits me now'. He died soon afterwards, on 7 July 1930.

The greatest and most glorious adventure

At his memorial service, held on 13 July in the Albert Hall, an empty chair was placed next to Jean, his widow. 6,000 people crammed in, many out of respect but most, perhaps, in the anticipation of a memorial service with a difference – an appearance from the man himself. They were not to be disappointed. After the usual sombre service, a woman admired by Conan Doyle for her qualities as a medium, Estelle Roberts, took to the stage. Proceedings now resembled a spiritualist stage show as she passed on messages of comfort from the other side to members of her audience. After thirty minutes or so, she turned to the empty chair and shouted, 'He is here.'

Only she, as the medium, could see him and, later, she said that Conan Doyle had been there throughout congratulating her on her performance. Speaking to Lady Jean, Roberts said, 'I have a message for you from Arthur.' She whispered a few words in Lady Jean's ear.

What those words were, Lady Jean never said and we will never know, but she smiled and took obvious comfort from them.

11 November 1920
The Burial of the Unknown Warrior

On 11 November 1920, two years after the armistice that ended the First World War, the Unknown Warrior was buried in London's Westminster Abbey in a deeply sombre ceremony that caught the mood of a nation, still reeling in grief following four years of war.

In 1916, the vicar of Margate in Kent, the Reverend David Railton, (a recipient of the Military Cross) was stationed as a padre on the Western Front near the French village of Armentières on the Belgian border when he noticed a temporary grave with the inscription, 'An Unknown British Soldier'. Moved by this simple epitaph, he initially suggested the notion to the British wartime commander-in-chief, Sir Douglas Haig that one fallen man, unknown in name or rank, should represent *all* those who died during the war who had no known grave. In August 1920, having received no response from Haig, Railton muted the idea to Herbert Ryle, the Dean of Westminster, who, in turn, passed it onto Buckingham Palace.

Initially, the king, George V, was not enthusiastic about the proposal; not wanting to re-open the healing wound of national grief but was persuaded into the idea by the prime minister, David Lloyd-George.

On 7 November 1920, the remains of six (some sources state four) unidentified British soldiers were exhumed – one each from six different battlefields (Aisne, Arras, Cambrai, Marne, Somme and Ypres). The six corpses were transported to a chapel in the village of St Pol, near Ypres, where they were each laid out on a stretcher and covered by the Union flag. There, in the company of a padre (not Rev Railton), a blindfolded officer entered the chapel and touched one of the bodies.

The following morning, chaplains of the Church of England, the Roman Catholic Church and Non-Conformist churches held a service for the chosen soldier. Placed in a plain coffin, the Unknown Warrior was taken back on a train to England via Boulogne. At Boulogne, the coffin was kept overnight in the town's castle, a guard of honour keeping vigil.

A British Warrior

On the morning of the 9 November, the coffin was placed in a larger casket made from wood, three inches thick, taken from an oak tree in the gardens of London's Hampton Court Palace. Mounted on the side of the coffin, a 16th century sword from the collection at the Tower of London especially chosen by George V. Draped over the casket, the Union flag, which had been used by Rev Railton as an altar cloth during the war. (The flag, known as the Padre's Flag, now hangs in St George's Chapel within Westminster Abbey). The coffin plate bore the inscription: 'A British Warrior who fell in the Great War

1914-1918 for King and Country'.

The procession through the town of Boulogne, led by a thousand French schoolchildren and accompanied by solemn military music, took the casket to the town's harbour. There it was met by Marshal Ferdinand Foch, the Allies' wartime supreme commander, before being transported across the English Channel to Dover on board the HMS *Verdun* (named after the French battle).

A train transported the casket from Dover to London. The body was afforded pomp and ceremony at every stage of its journey – processions and gun salutes. Crowds of people, braving the cold and the rain and clad in mourning, turned out at every station to watch the train pass through carrying its precious cargo. Groups of boy scouts played the 'Last Post', guards of honour formed on station platforms. Every bridge was filled with silent spectators, saluting as the train passed beneath.

The train pulled into Victoria Station at 8.32 on the evening of 10 November, arriving at platform eight, greeted by a mass of people. Many were in tears. Today, next to platform eight, a plaque (pictured above), unveiled in 1998, commemorates the occasion. The coffin remained on the train overnight, under guard, and surrounded by wreaths so large and so heavy that it took four men to lift each one into place.

The Procession

On the morning of 11 November 1920, exactly two years on from Armistice Day, eight soldiers placed the coffin on a horse-drawn gun carriage, borne by six black stallions. A nineteen-gun salute signalled the start of the procession. It was nine thirty in the morning. Dense, silent crowds lined the streets. Cars and all traffic were banned from the roads for the day. Muffled drums accompanied Chopin's *Funeral March* as the procession slowly wound its way pass Hyde Park Corner and onto The Mall and into Whitehall, where the king laid a wreath of red roses and bay leaves on top of the casket before unveiling the newly-erected Cenotaph.

The twelve pallbearers included field marshals, air chief marshals and various generals, among them Douglas Haig. The king, as chief mourner, and his entourage then followed the cortège to Westminster Abbey. Behind them, four hundred ex-servicemen walked four abreast, and, behind them, a mass of black-clad mourners, men, women and children. Soldiers lining the roads bowed their heads and reversed arms as the cortège passed. Waiting at Westminster Abbey was a guard of honour consisting of 100 holders of the Victoria Cross and 100 women who had lost both their husbands and all of their sons during the war.

The Service

The brief service, which included at eleven o'clock a two minute silence, was recorded. The recording became the first electrical recording ever sold to the public. Following the service, the coffin was lowered into the grave, 'amongst the kings'. The king sprinkled the coffin with earth brought back from the Western Front.

In the week that followed, some 1,300,000 people visited the Abbey to pay their respects to the Unknown Warrior.

On 18 November, a week after the service, the grave was filled in using 100 sandbags of French soil, and covered with a stone slab with the simple inscription, 'A British warrior who fell in the Great War 1914-1918 for King and Country. Greater love hath no man like this.'

The following year, on 11 November 1921, the stone was replaced by a slab of Belgium marble, seven feet by four feet three, and six inches thick, and fully inscribed in capitals with text composed by the Dean of Westminster.

On 21 October 1921, General John Pershing of the US army awarded the Unknown Warrior the Congressional Medal of Honor, the USA's highest military honour. The medal was framed and now hangs on a nearby pillar. In return, the US Unknown Soldier, who was interred in the Arlington National Cemetery on 11 November 1921, was awarded the Victoria Cross.

In 1923, the future Queen Mother married the future King George VI at Westminster Abbey. As the new bride left the Abbey, she placed her wedding bouquet on the grave of the Unknown Warrior, starting a tradition that is still practiced today by all royal brides.

In 1993, Australia buried their unknown soldier, Canada in 2000 and, most recently, New Zealand in 2004.

Images and Disclaimers

All the images used in this book are, as far as I can ascertain, in the public domain. If I have mistakenly used an image that is not in the public domain, please let me know at felix@historyinanhour.com and I shall remove / replace the offending item as soon as I can.

Also, while I have taken great care to ensure every fact and figure is correct, there are a lot of them and I am only human. Therefore, if you spot a mistake, please just let me know without exposing me too publicly, and I will check and amend if necessary. Thank you.

Complete Series:

The Clever Teens' Guide to World War One
The Clever Teens' Guide to World War Two
The Clever Teens' Guide to the Russian Revolution
The Clever Teens' Guide to Nazi Germany
The Clever Teens' Guide to the Cold War

The Clever Teens' Tales From World War One
The Clever Teens' Tales From World War Two
The Clever Teens' Tales From the Cold War

Printed in Great Britain
by Amazon